New Roof in October

poems by

Elizabeth Wix

New Roof in October

Whoever chose green shingles for such a house?
underneath the green
lie gray and rotted wooden tiles
and something in between (a blue like slate)
all of it flying!
smashing hosta and pachysandra
rhododendron and wisteria
the beams bare to the sky again
after eighty years imprisonment

they're ripping the roof off the house
and the wind and rain at night
beat upon the attic walls
and pails fill up with speckled juice
leeched from the darkened beams
tarpaulins flap and bicker
as the cold
invades the upper rooms

there is something about this attack
this abandon and rearrangement
this smiting of all that protected us

the attic door rattles as the night
eager to enter (but unhanded)
leaps down the stairs and waits
not ten feet from our bed

they have taken all that kept us safe
from the moon's rays
and eyes in aeroplanes
and parts of stars cavorting down to earth

The Poem Hiding

At last!
in the linen basket
cornered
gotcha
thank god for that!
you're feeble, granted
but I'll take you out and prod you
pummel you
until you make the semblance of some sense
(six cigarettes, a cup of tea)
you're coming round, you ratty thing
sit up!
or else I'll put you in a drawer instead

October

The pumpkin patch was small suburban
        the track pure mud
        the celebration muted
we did not bend and touch the dirt
        have prickled vines tear at our hands
        see insects scatter

We decorate with stalks we did not sow
round fruits bedeck the porch
and lanterns glitter demon-like
        the eyes now watch us
        teeth lopsided grin

They know our folly
pity us
        who did not lie in mud the autumn long
        and feel the first cold wind
        nor watch the moon the night time through
but came one afternoon
        and paid
        to play at husbandry

A Visit

This isn't what you expected
nevertheless this is it
you know I had always intended
something a little more posh
where the faucets all worked
and the debris was decorative
with dados and cornices
and the neighbors somewhat genteel
with porches wholly attached
lacking the thundering noises
when next-doors' trucks draw out

I apologize for the spiders
and the plaster falling in heaps
and the fact that the fire whistle screeches
and the bedcovers scarcely match

But the china's all Spode
and somewhere a tea pot (pure silver)
lurks with bonbon dishes in paper
and there are all sorts of flowers in vases
two children
two cats
one hamster
a husband
a colonial TV like George Washington watched
an absence of time
large numbers of books
and your friendship these last twenty years

The Journey of the Magi

You ask me who the Wise Men were
Balthazar Caspar Melchior
who journeyed from the East -- or did not
who travelled through Judea (then Palestine)
bearing gold and frankincense and myrrh
who bypassed Samarkand
(perhaps met Ozymandias himself)

certainly they lived once
the men with magic names had flesh
circulatory systems
indigestion perhaps flat feet
bunions even
eyes that sand got in
itches
a burning need to pee or spit

they've had long years now to get over all that
to stop being more than incantations
gateways and doors we open up on long dark afternoons

Caspar I think it was who had black skin
wide lips and jewels cascading from his horse's mane
Melchior surely was an alchemist
transforming dross to gold
and Balthazar --too weighted by his name
was merely Balthazar
a dandy
conscious even then
that looks will get you mentioned aeons on
in some dim room beige-walled and dull
where light is muted by the shades
and spitballs sit upon the floor.

Eastbury Manor Nursing Home

I think you're overdoing things to call it home
monstrous Victorian manor house
hard by the church
whose immemorial yews got blasted by the storm
and broke the wall between the two

Does it make it any easier
this dissolution of bounds and categories
between the living and the dead?

Your body in this house
(one window overlooks the lake)
your soul contained
in an anteroom papered with mottled skin

How still the bodies lie next door!
(one window overlooks the graves)

How strong the wind that hurled the limb
that howling night
and tore the turf
allowing access to the quiet ground

JDW 1911-1979

My father had gone blackberrying
when the air was clear and warm
and the fruit he gathered lingered on a saucer that was cracked.
(Is there some etiquette I wonder
about food picked by the dead?)

My father died considerately
between breakfast time and lunch.
His last words: Don't cancel Alfriston.
After that, I suppose, they broke his ribs
I didn't ask,
but washed the clothes they sent back
before my mother could see them.
My brother lit a bonfire
a long way from the house.
I catalogue the things:
the cuff-links, shiny bottomed suits
Masonic robes and collar studs
the patent leather shoes for dancing
the cravats and cummerbunds.

My mother wailed: He wasn't old
as she snatched the letters from me.
I bought flowers for my father
who valued function over form
who painted the gate bile green and loved it
who wept in movies
made bad jokes and laughed himself
whose probity was absolute
who sang too loud
who showed my poems to his friends
to whom the lilies (out of season)
the pinks and larkspur would mean nothing.
I added rosemary from his garden
and lavender from his hedge.

Letter

After he was dead
I got a letter from my father
saying how many cake crumbs he'd found down the back
of the armchair we left at his house
and how he'd returned the crib and the playpen
we'd borrowed for our son
to Enid Chelmer
and how that warm September afternoon
there were enough ripe blackberries
for a good pie at every meal

he recalled writing to me at school each week
now he'd do the same
but this time to America
couching his love
in daily life
the common round
the trivial task
the plans for fishing
dinner
church

written in his neat familiar hand
speaking to me now through twenty years
(our son now grown to adulthood)
recalling the benison of him
who wrote no more letters to me

New Restaurant on New York Avenue

Before they bought fresh paint and nails
the stairs were rickety and vile
the downstairs OTB
and up above lived Jon-Jon
lovely child whose vast brown eyes
and humor overwhelmed
his lack of grace at meals
Jon-Jon whose grandpa's Cadillac
took up a block
who said "Don't worry!"
as he swept my son to movies
once (in ice) to puppets
once to Halloween
up above the OTB
lived Jon-Jon Maurice and the rest
with beer cans music mattresses
more rats than young boys dream of
these virile uncles young and bold
who ribbed me on the telephone
wronged husbands left and right
and laughed
wore knives upon their belts
one night before they thought of paint
when Jon-Jon slept protected by his dreams
there came a cuckold up the stairs
whose knife blade glittered in the moon
so Maurice took a shotgun
blew away his head
now Claudie asks me to climb up those stairs
eat in that room
                    whose walls are washed of blood

Some Pain

I tore the picture from the paper
      three days before I lost my job
you remember it probably
      (for who could not)

the man squats
thin knees angled upwards
      his face expressionless
      his daughter at his feet
      she and another child

the man smooths back his daughter's hair
      and her white socks are turned back
      for the last time
      neatly at the ankle

The Poetry Course

Poems by the ream!
by the yard!
Order them now!
(no rhymes --they're out of date
quaint
unsuitable)

Order something dashing
vibrant
infinitely memorable.

Feeling?
well, that's extra
it doesn't come so easily
Beggar boys are two a penny
cripples gratis
widows could be worked in if you wanted

Death?
there's been a run on that of late
Love?
well, if you must
(I prefer to think that's private
)
So we're left with
teacups spiders' webs
(small details only)
unless you want the larger vein
(annihilation Gorbochev Chernobyl Reagan)

I'll give you what you want
I'm practiced at tailoring
a tuck here
expansion there
some local color
enough to lighten a dark corner
some words to match the color of your couch?
to please you I'll turn somersaults
avoid cliche
 eschew pastiche
(I'll even praise the down of peaches

sunsets beaches)
but leave me out of it

Antique Shop

Daguerreotype post mortem
translates: dead baby
abed in profile
I looked of course
I couldn't not
forehead rounded
sparse soft hair
four weeks perhaps or months
no more

nice little red morocco gilded case
a curiosity
for sale to anyone

B with pneumonia at nine months
brown suit white face
eyes fast shut
I took his photo then
and have it still
have him in flesh and breath
no neat morocco case (gold clasp)
no cash to buy that other mother's pain
nor wish to know it

Your Room Opposite the Arthur Murray School of Dance

No longer do I weep in airports late at night
feel ghostly hands caress my thighs
nor wear black swirling capes
and trace
the beatings of my heart in burnt sienna ink
No more!
I buy my cards at Hallmark
shop judiciously
at discount stores
and wear what's least offensive

I abhor romance
eat tuna fish
and dream
of when
the cobblestones were wet with rain
the window crack reflected light
and you were om and brahman too

the night was black
your blankets blood
and they reflected on your ceiling
danced the night away
circling and circling
plumply
cosily
those clumsy clerks and housewives
I jeered at
       and became

Cowardice

We're adept at committing adultery
geniuses at it in fact
if eye contact constitutes passion
and phone calls make up the act

If avoiding the truth is a virtue
they'd award us the Pulitzer Prize
we touch hands so lightly at parties
but lust for a clamping of thighs

You say you find me remarkable
I likewise find you the same
but neither of us wishes to publicly
do anything likely to maim

I despise this mode of behavior
I think it silly and vain
instead of wild animal thrashings
we get mere avoidance of pain

Instead of clandestine meetings
and beatings of fond hearts entwined
we go in for dull rarified pleasure
that only goes on in the mind

Invitation

You may enter my house
for surely I'll invite you in
we'll sit awhile and talk
but first you note the bicycles
that clutter up the hall
(first augers of my children's leaving)
but now they force a sort of life
I never realized I'd know.

You see the plants -- green burgeoning
my husband's pets
(I only grow wild things and words)

How should I detail what you see?
the laundry basket, rubber gloves
the piles of students' books
the calendar
my caste

Or did you come to find
what lies behind the front
the half hour snatched
between the mother and the fount of rules?

the curving road beside the water
the sun so stately rising
(a spectacle not stopped for)
the pleasure found in faces
the day holds in abeyance?

At other times the music spills into the woods
the blue heron stands knee deep in mud
I feel the wind bat at the torpor of the trees
(the cottage sheltered like a fairy tale)
the weight and stillness of the snow
that renders known land strange and magic

If this is peace and poetry

it's delved for
hunted like the Snark
the minutes hewn too precious to be squandered
but mined as gifts
and held as talismen
against the dull encroach of worlds
where clauses, conflicts, competence hold sway

After the Accident

Necrosis is death of tissue
skin and flesh turned perfectly black
(blacker far than a coal-hued African)
but not glistening
knee flesh attached by coarse stitches
as flat black as St. Clare's --
centuries old
in her cold tomb in Assisi
The ex-fix with seven sharp pins
is pure Sebastian surely
poor arrow-shot youth
(how well I learned my icons in some past life)
now we learn a new vocabulary
more suited to this one
(did Foley and Hickman give their names gladly
to tubes of lesser torture?)
he becomes very nearly some secular saint
attended revered
cheeks hollowed in mortification
(the beard grown in nearly Christ-like!)
I wash feet in a bowl so immaculately wrapped
that to reveal it seems sacrilege almost
some merit in service
these lowly acts of supplication
tending (one hopes) to the greater good
the rough skin of the soles
detaches
flakes
falls into saline
new vulnerable skin echoes soul
unused to the light
bare as new life
                       stripped open and secretless

Childhood

a poem in several parts

1
Herongate

I am making a list of people to write about
a cast of characters:
Ivy and Tim Bullen whose name a corruption of Boleyn
(tragic queen with six fingers on either hand)
Mrs. Dickerson -- the old-lady-with-no-stockings
and Mr. De'ath

The Reverend G. Porter
The Reverend Ray Powell
Mrs. Boxall whose shop gave short measure
Mr. Ablin silent baker
Gwen Elliott whose grandiose house
had a porticoed front door and green tiles like a
villa in Spain
Miss Chaplin a dwarf who smocked dresses

They are most of them dead now
ghosts who lived in a village
small speck on a map
insignificant place
my dreams turn to
mythic as Parnassus
as lost as the ark
nether world of lost passion
a remarkable place
Iwander at will

2

Tankerton

Granny had a bullet in her neck for forty years
we could touch it if we asked her
snuggling up in her divan bed
slipping our arms carefully
round the back of her head
"Lunch !" she'd said and her brothers, shooting rabbits
shot her instead
Granny had blue and white mugs
honey gritty at the bottom
made us wear beach shoes, rubber with colored swirls like oil in puddles
we walked through dark municipal gardens with neatly tended beds
up a hill to where the graves were and the light
I had a present every day from a shop where the counters were trestle tables
all pale wood underneath
Sharp's toffees and popper beads to chew
and a plastic dagger whose blade went in
we visit a man who buys antiques
a crook my father says
who gives me little china jugs
takes Granny's things
but not the clock in the hall with the sun's face
and the moon's
and a lady riding on a horse forever
in the attic a rocker like a swan
no wonder when my mother said to come home
                      I thought I'd rather stay.

3

Grandpa at Thorpe Bay

The room was dim and smelled of camphor
he sat in the dark
in a wheelchair and his breath came funnily
I allowed him to kiss me
only because of the box of chocolate mints high up on the mantle
where I couldn't reach

downstairs Oliver made pennies come out of his ears
a treat but frightening
I knew I was being tricked
was tricked
the money coming from nowhere

4
Thorndon Park

The fountain with the lions on it
never played but once
and the tulip tree bloomed once in seven years
which we never saw for all our looking

the way through the woods closed in
with birches whose branches whipped near my eyes
and the carriage ride once wide
now almost lost
led to the chapel
hidden now almost
last resting place of Papists
servants
dogs
where a woman
bent double
scrubbed at the flagstoned floor
black and white squares that the colored windows painted
magenta in spots

the man-made lake
with the brick arched boat house
where my parents skated once before the war
when the water
froze solid as it never did now
had a landing craft for fishing
with tilted deck
green slimed inside
that smelled of Normandy beaches

deep in the lake
sunk
where we couldn't get at it

was a plane with the enemy pilot still inside

at the edge of the lake black shells like clams

pearlescent inside gleaming like mother of pearl
how icy the water
how red our hands searching for them in winter

5

Dam Busters March

You jump thump off the toy cupboard
onto the floor
flying suddenly through the air like the bombs smashing the dam
it is very merry you can do it for hours
and the house shakes like it should

for artistic performances
fairies witches giants and stuff like that
we charge threepence and Mummy and the Bullens pay
though it's less fun really than bombs

6

Chickenpox

Fetid hot sheets with toast crumbs in them
the doctor's stethoscope cold on my chest
and not allowed to go outside for days
and trying never to swallow at all
the thermometer takes almost a thousand hours
and still it's 99.8 or 102
Mummy flicks it down with her wrist
but won't let me
try it ever
because all the little beads of mercury
will escape and wander

waking up in the night to take medicine
and pills
which even crushed up into sugar taste bitter
hot pillow turned to the cold side
lasts three minutes only
and why won't you come upstairs to talk to me
not leave me here alone for ever
darling don't pick at your spots
you'll get scars
do leave them alone
and the wind in the aspen leaves flutters like rain

7

Hospital

A child's cot when I have a bed at home
barred in
trapped
milk on my cornflakes
I don't have that at home

a playroom at the other end through glass
where I'm never allowed to go
though some people are

my brother gives me a fairy doll
bought with his own money my mother says

the days she doesn't come I cry and cry
and cry
and Oliver sits by the bed -- that child's cot
and I cry

8

Daddy

Daddy buys red boots with fur in
(because he doesn't know we wear plain shoes)
dries my hair too roughly with a towel by the drawing room fire
(Mummy would have made finger waves)

reads *Alice Through the Looking Glass*
and leads us for long walks by the lake
beats Muffin when he runs away
eats Patum Paternum on crunchy toast

 sings *MacNamara's Band, Tit Willow, The Mountains of Morne*
has a mustache that scratches and gives Daddy-tucks

hands the plate at church
(where his position is second only to the Rev. G. Porter)
people have carved their initials in the black varnished wood
under the shelf you put your hymn book on
and four angels trumpeting heaven surround the figure of a
forgiving Christ
with arms outstretched in stained glass and rather ugly
(This is my Beloved Son in Whom I am Well Pleased)

9

Mummy

is simply so much there
that I don't see her often
she wears V-necked shirt-waister dresses her skin brown in the V
(it's comfortable under her dress)
when she kneels to brush my hair we're almost the same height
she walks me to school telling stories
through the woods past the piggery (which stinks when the
wind's from the east)
she has ladies to tea
we eat lunch in the dining room
Rose in the kitchen
why?
her dressing table mirror has three parts
(so you can see your nose sticking out sideways)
three lipsticks in a drawer that smells of spilled powder
(Coty -- the round box with the fans on)
she powders her nose before Daddy comes home
wears the perfume I make from rose petals steeped in the sun
on the red front door porch tiles
wears a brooch like a glittering fish Peter bought her in
Chelmsford
even though she and I know it's not real jewels

sings *Now the Day is Over* and *nigh nigh*
out of tune
says her prayers night and morning
kneeling on the hard wood boards by her bed

10

The Fifth of November

Guy Fawkes was a Roman Catholic
who tried to blow up parliament
they caught him in the cellar
and broke his fingers first
made him sign a confession (wobbly handed)
then burnt him

he burns each year on top of piles of leaves and rubbish
(he was a Catholic after all)
bangers
sparklers
jumping jacks which jump in your boot and burn you too

Catherine Wheels (which fail to spin) on posts
and rockets falling red and gold

bangers to eat and not-very-baked baked potatoes in their jackets
days afterwards we sniff dead fireworks
picked up from damp grass

Christmas

In a tin in the larder
a robin a snowman and a thatched cottage with
ancient royal icing fused like stone

in a cardboard box in the study
Christmas tree balls in yellowed tissue paper
two plastic bells one red and one blue
and flashing lights like candles that flop sideways

bought from shops thin strips of multicolored paper for paper
chains

holly behind the pictures
a limp clump of mistletoe in the hall
tangerines on the fruit stand
and sticky dates in an oval box with a camel on it

and the cards!
so many cards
(I can open the ones that say 'and family' on them)

three trees from Kent
ours the rector's the church's
with translucent resin stinky pure
that sticks to your fingers

and not being able to sleep at all on Christmas Eve
kicking at the bottom of the bed all night
(Dad's fishing sock awaits treasure)
then the stocking presents in yesterday's paper
(and bits of paper crumpled to round out the shape)
an apple dull as dull
a duller orange
then chocolate money sticking to foil
at the very toe

a silver sixpence

crackers at lunch with labels that fall off
and paper hats that slip over your eyes
or else tear along the join
jokes so old Methuselah jeered at them

and so much church you thought you would die of it
all ye faithful
joyful and triumphant
for ever and ever

and it never snowed though it should have done
with the air so stale and heavy
the sky colored like lead

12

House

You step down into the larder which is always cool
has hooks on the ceiling for hanging game
the floor in the kitchen is black and white stone
Rose kneels on a hot water bottle when she scrubs it
her bottom round in the air

in the hall is a brass stand with umbrellas and sticks
with a shiny picture beaten in to it
and a cupboard with mackintoshes and boots
if you cover your face with the coats you're invisible
and no one can find you

the soap in the downstairs lavatory is shiny and see through
and the stink of cigarette smoke
and a bakelite ashtray

our bathroom is narrow and yellow
has frosted glass windows
and the washing machine with the wringer

in my room a fox's mask stares at me glassily
though none of us hunt
and a picture called *Joy in the Morning*
with a girl dancing dressed in yellow
arms uplifted on top of a hill with rabbits and foxes
and *Awakening* by Bessie Pease Gutman
with a fat baby (not me) her hair is too dark it might be a boy

13

Garden

In spring beneath the silver birch
a feeble clump of snowdrops
beyond the fruit cage rhododendrons to make tunnels in
and houses
with rusted pots and pans to cook in

across the drive a laurel with shiny leaves
by the kennels the bush of butterflies --
buddleia which smells of something strange
then a rockery
a herbaceous border
rose beds
wall flowers along the crazy paving path
and lupins in the hundreds just
like beside the train
and two may trees whose flowers drop
so sharp they stab my feet

14
1955

On winter Friday afternoons
let off from school
we drove past flat dead fields
buildings bombed and dank
and gypsy caravans
saw tinkers' children slimy-nosed and vile
make faces at us
reached the black waters of the Thames
where ferry boats might sink
beneath the eerie call of hooters
and screams of circling gulls

Ships left from Tilbury
sailing to the ends of the world
we merely crossed from Essex into Kent
(at Gravesend they advertised a dozen kinds of beer)
flying boats bobbed at Rochester
where front gardens of mean stuccoed homes
grew monkey-puzzle trees
(too complex for an ape to fathom
my mother said
lace curtains hide lives you needn't know about)

In towns themselves
soot-coated fanlit doors had knockers that changed
at dusk to Marley's face
and closeted clerks in rooms
warmed by one coal perhaps
or none

In open land barbed wire was strung
to closet out the Hun
pill-boxes faced the leaden sea
and radar towers turned on
below gray skies bereft of planes

The beaches crunched beneath our feet
our thighs in woolen leggings chapped and raw
the cold waves slapped at shingle
we skipped stones
counted their hops a moment
saw them swallowed up
the tide turned somewhere further out
our ears strained to hear the sound of guns

My life closed twice before its close --Emily Dickinson

Twice only have I met my soul
and talked with it quite separate from me
twice only have I ceased to be
and flying free
whimpered for the earth

too shattering a revelation
too strange and strong a notion
to be and not to be
see bodies breath and motion
from far above and fearfully

how wild this spinning like a kite
unfettered diving in delight
now in and out
of substance form and shape
the room a map a battle rout
between the known and infinite

twice only has the bond been snapped
between the real and wonderment
I keep it trapped
enshackled weighted down and bound
a curious atonement

Untitled

I allow
tannin and nicotine
sharp pencils
the backs of envelopes
slamming of doors
DO NOT DISTURB ON PAIN OF DEATH

I hate writing
always have
love words
as much as anything
love thought
creation
silence
white virgin paper
pain

I want to tell you everything
so when I'm gone
you will recall the fact
I meant to write
but loved you better
did both as well as I was able
both imperfectly

Laurie Moon

the very name!
the princess of a thousand dreams
whose bed is canopied and white
whose Barbie dolls are put away
so safely for her daughter

Laurie Moon
whose sweetness countermands all blame
whose teeth are white
whose waist is slim
whose grades are adequate
who then became Homecoming Queen
Oh Princess of a Thousand Dreams -- now Queen
whose hair is golden
whose nails so pink and picturesque
tap out the price at Genovese

what's gnawing at this idyll's heart?
Instead of loving Ken
you chose a boy of flesh and blood
some temper
and no cash
whose dad ran off
whose mother works
who cannot shower you with pearls
and emeralds and gold
your mother would approve of
So princess of the pompom
smile and suburb
you split between your passion for his flesh
and Ken and Barbie and the rest
Your queenly pillow wet with tears
your perfect heart past mending

April 2000

not having fought anything ever
he would not attack his death
but slipped into it leisurely
letting his breath
come shallower shallower
until at last it swallowed him up
washed his flesh clean of sentience
washed him clean out of himself
leaving a pale fish
with open snorer's mouth
beached on white sheets

Painting

He makes a mix of images
culled from long days spent noting how
light falls on trees and tracks and faces
places of no inherent charm or much

this latest one
from left to right
has first a subway rider -- male
reading *the daily news* perhaps
he travels slyly into the next frame
where choice brings him to the beach
flat shoreline where the sand meets sea
(the waves break further out)
or up to where the subway car itself
untenanted
is misted noxious green

next a woman's eye downcast
a large eye turned in upon itself
then water that reflects the sun and tall thin masts
of ships we cannot see

last a gray swath rising to palest pale
a patch of ostwald red
that's all
a jumble of the random now called art
to deconstruct as we think fit
each element a fractured part
of what is really there
to take apart and reconstruct
dissolve transmute
seek meaning if we must

August 7

Sweet little girl at the travel agent's
(plumply pretty but unused to disaster)
picks up the phone with wavering hand
and says what she must
what she can
there's been a terrible accident she says
he's asking for you
his leg's half off
at Sleepy's by the mall

I'll come immediately I say
as our daughter stands aghast
claudie who picked up the poisoned phone
knows disaster when she sees it
weeps
clutching the stairs
at just past noon on Monday morning
bright and clear
cool for the start of August
the best of days

we were always waiting for this to happen
this call
shattering the inertia of long days of light
now dark
the stomach first reacts
the brain (on hold) thinks
what to do?
thinks: he is not dead
not that at least
for that we give our thanks and praise

shout to other cars please let us pass
there's been an accident
his leg's half off
see flashing lights and run through traffic holding up my hand
as the ambulance turns across the street

His vital signs are good the paramedic says

as the blood dries on the road a pool if it
congealing at the edges

the cop asks: you want his things?
the bloody gloves which smells
the boots cut off
I pick them up and cast them down
what do you want to do with the bike?
my god I'm mother come to tidy up
you throw the fucking thing away I say

the helicopter rises in the air
turns
is gone whirling through the air and westward
the policeman winks at me
we write the address on the back of my checkbook
and go
into the long day's glare
the long straight road
turn south

you have insurance, of course, they ask
you want to see him?
yes he asked for me
still asks and clasps my hand in his
lies on a gurney
surrounded by people wearing green

but the leg!
I've been hurt he says
she hit me
he's wheeled away
you understand these papers hastily drawn up?
I do not understand but sign
sit on a hard backed chair in a green dim room
they look me straight in the eye
but he will not die I say?
his vital signs are good
no threat to life
his limbs don't matter anyway
life only is all I ask

doctors are paged for amputation

simple
straightforward
a hacksaw to the bone
no need to rush
but then he moved his toes
one tells him swallow this -- a tube
another twists the leg
a third with scalpel to the navel cuts
no solace here no opiate
but pain

four hours at least
no need to sit
buy shoes and chinese food and magazines
and wait
and wait
relive my mother buying towels a thousand years ago
when I was then my daughter's age
and my father didn't die

now I become the one who waits
tragedienne
mock heroine
the center (almost)
of attention
who asks for tea
is bought it in a styrene cup
you mustn't pay
this is the least I can do
the magazines are glossy dull
concerning lives I'll never lead
in Highland castles daubed in plaid

in six hours the surgeon reappears
sits down on cracked slashed naugahyde
orange of course --what else?
he says he's Persian looks rumpled old
is courtly
of the old school
scrabbles in his pocket for a notebook

my husband tells me he's been hurt
in recovery with dim lights and tubes and

things that buzz and soon I'm led away
at nine at night
light gone
nick comes to take me home
provides a shoulder cigarette
a small brown pill crushed up in liquid
I tell the children everything is fine
to go to sleep
                        and go to sleep myself

Villeroy and Boch

They reap the corn two centuries ago
in some hot european field
where two men stand
bent slightly over scythes
and women stoop to gather what's been cut
it was ever thus

this tasteful scene
congeals beneath my weetabix
in monochrome
(bone china
dishwasher safe)
atop a polished table

the sweat! the smell!
the hours under scalding sun
I'd hate to be a peasant then
broad-fingered, ignorant and numb
to everything but aching back and shoulders' burn
I'd long to loll beside the cows
in shade beneath the heavy trees
I wouldn't care to look *charmant*
to decorate a dish
my labor turned to prettiness

Book Jacket

I always look
at the poet's picture on the back of books
you can never tell
when you look in the newspaper
if the picture is perpetrator victim hero
or merely someone's uncle who discovered the body

why should it be any better with poets
who may have buck teeth
ears that stick out
or mesmerizing eyes
cause by strabismus astigmatism or mere vanity

tilt your head just so
the photographer said
and get rid of the glasses

the inner grace isn't written
here
plain on the cover
but still I look anyway
curious to see what package the thoughts come in
to glean from flesh and bone
a message to alter the text

Made in the USA
Lexington, KY
03 April 2012